CAPTAIN FACT's

CREEPY-CRAWLY ADVENTURE

BY
KNIFE & PACKER

EGMONT

KNIFE & PACKER FACT!

KNIFE AND PACKER'S SCARIEST CREEPY-CRAWLY ENCOUNTER
WAS WHEN A HUMUNGOUS WASP SNUCK IN THROUGH THE
OFFICE WINDOW ONE SUMMER. IT SET UP HOME IN THEIR ONE
AND ONLY PENCIL CASE AND THEY WERE FORCED TO WORK IN
THE BATHROOM!

First published in Great Britain in 2004
by Egmont Books Limited, 239 Kensington High Street, London W8 6SA

Text and illustrations copyright © 2004 Knife and Packer
The moral rights of the authors have been asserted.

ISBN 1 4052 0834 1

3 5 7 9 10 8 6 4 2

A CIP catalogue record for this title is available
from the British Library

Printed and bound in Great Britain

CONTENTS

1   PRESIDENT IN PERIL   7

2   THAT SHRINKING FEELING   19

3   BEDBUGS BITE BACK   29

4   BUZZ OFF!   37

5   POND LIFE   45

6   THAT STING THING   53

7   RUMBLE IN THE JUNGLE   63

8   BLUNDER DOWN UNDER   73

9   BIT ON THE BOT!   81

10   AND NOW THE WEATHER...   91

STAR

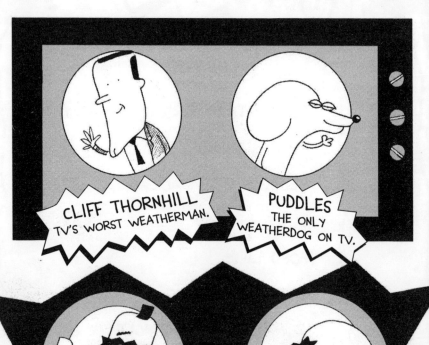

CLIFF THORNHILL
TV'S WORST WEATHERMAN.

PUDDLES
THE ONLY
WEATHERDOG ON TV.

CAPTAIN FACT
THE WORLD'S FIRST
INFORMATION SUPERHERO.

KNOWLEDGE
CAPTAIN FACT'S
FAITHFUL SIDEKICK.

RING...

LUCY
HEAD OF MAKE-UP AND CLIFF'S BEST FRIEND.

THE BOSS
HE'S SCARY!

PROFESSOR MINISCULE
HEAD OF THE FACT CAVE AND THE BRAINS BEHIND MISSIONS.

FACTORELLA
PROFESSOR MINISCULE'S DAUGHTER AND ALL-ROUND WHIZZ-KID.

CHAPTER 1
PRESIDENT IN PERIL

IT WAS A boiling hot summer's day and TV's worst weatherman Cliff Thornhill and his co-presenter Puddles the dog were enjoying the annual office picnic.

Well, they would have been enjoying it if it weren't for all the pesky insects. And the fact that Cliff had got the weather forecast wrong again.

'Look at this, Puddles,' moaned Cliff. 'There's flies in the fizzy drinks, wasps on the waffles . . .'

'And I've got ants all over my apple-pie-flavoured dog biscuits!' said Puddles.

As Cliff, Puddles and the rest of the studio staff struggled to fight off the local wildlife, one person was having a great time . . . the Boss. He had a personal mosquito net set up so there were no creepy-crawlies on him or his groaning table of treats. With a chocolate éclair in each hand he was happily dancing to his favourite radio show in a bug-free environment . . .

LA LA-OLÉ!

Suddenly the music stopped.

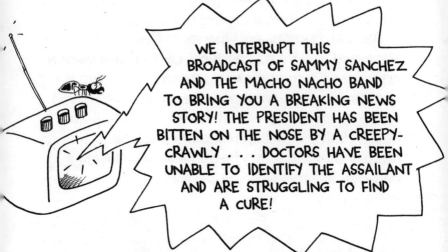

WE INTERRUPT THIS BROADCAST OF SAMMY SANCHEZ AND THE MACHO NACHO BAND TO BRING YOU A BREAKING NEWS STORY! THE PRESIDENT HAS BEEN BITTEN ON THE NOSE BY A CREEPY-CRAWLY . . . DOCTORS HAVE BEEN UNABLE TO IDENTIFY THE ASSAILANT AND ARE STRUGGLING TO FIND A CURE!

'Right!' yelled the Boss. 'This is the biggest news story in decades! Everyone back to the studio! I want to see the best news programme ever! I'll see you up there just as soon as I've finished my cream doughnut, strawberry cheesecake, banana split, chocolate-chip cookies, fudge sundae . . .'

'Do you think the President will pull through?' asked Lucy, Cliff's friend from the Make-up Department, as they rushed to the newsroom.

'I'm sure he's being seen by the best doctors in the world,' said Cliff, blushing. Cliff always went a bit mushy when Lucy was around.

'Where are you going?' asked Lucy. 'Aren't you going to watch the story unfold?'

'Erm, no,' gulped Cliff as he opened the door to his office. 'We've got to, er, start preparing the evening weather forecast. Apparently it's going to, er, be hot tomorrow.'

'That's strange,' thought Lucy, 'another crisis and another disappearing act by Cliff and Puddles. And why were they wearing raincoats?'

As soon as Cliff had shut the office door he threw off his raincoat and looked at Puddles. The two of them exclaimed:

THIS IS A MISSION FOR CAPTAIN FACT

And with that Puddles pulled the lever to reveal the pole to the Fact Cave.

11

CAPTAIN FACT

KNOWLEDGE

13

'Right, Knowledge,' said Captain Fact as they ran down the corridors of the Fact Cave, 'if we're going to save the President we're going to have to find out what bit him – and quickly. Only when we've pinpointed the creepy-crawly responsible will we be able to identify the cure. And it's not going to be easy. Ker-Fact! There are over one million different species of insects!'

'How bad can a creepy-crawly bite be?' asked Knowledge, 'I'm always getting bitten by fleas. A bit of ointment, a plaster and all the doggie chocs I can eat works every time.'

'I think you'll find that some creepy-crawlies are a lot more dangerous than fleas,' said Captain Fact, 'and they've got all kinds of weapons at their disposal.' Just then his knees began to knock . . .

KNOCK!

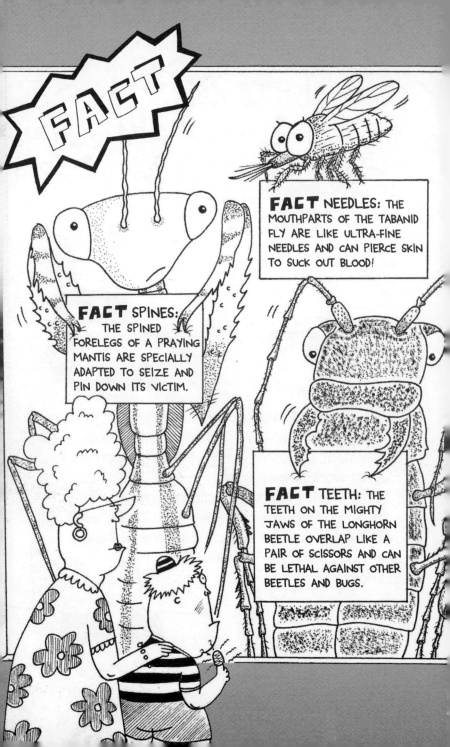

'That lot would have my fleas for breakfast!' said Knowledge nervously.

'Yes, and we're going to have to get up close and personal with a whole world of miniature monsters, if we're going to save the President,' said Captain Fact as the door to the Nerve Centre cranked open.

CHAPTER 2
THAT SHRINKING FEELING

'AH, CAPTAIN FACT and Knowledge. What kept you?' asked Professor Miniscule, the world's shortest genius. 'The President's condition is most worrying. It would appear the creepy-crawly bite has affected his brain. At first he was twitching and mumbling. Now he's barking in a high-pitched manner, rather like a Chihuahua. We have to get you out in the field searching for the creepy-crawly responsible as soon as possible . . .'

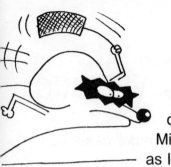

'Let's do it!' said Knowledge, trying to swat a bug that was scuttling in the direction of Professor Miniscule's lunch. 'Just as soon as I get this critter.'

'STOP!' screamed Professor Miniscule. 'That's no critter, that's Factorella!'

'Factorella?' inquired Captain Fact, 'but how did she get so tiny?'

'I shrunk her,' said Professor Miniscule matter-of-factly, 'with this – my latest invention, the Shrinkotron 2000. And I'm going to shrink *you*, so *you* can investigate creepy-crawlies from a worm's eye view.'

Taking careful aim at the mini Factorella, Professor Miniscule squinted down the viewfinder and squeezed the trigger on the Shrinkotron 2000. There was a bone-shuddering bang, a flash of blue light and there before them, back to her usual size, stood Factorella.

'Why did you un-shrink me, Dad?' asked Factorella. 'I thought *I* was going on the mission.'

'No, Factorella, you know fine well you're not old enough to go on missions,' said Professor Miniscule sternly. 'You've still got years and years of superhero training ahead of you. And anyway, we might need you in an emergency. Now, what's Factotum got for us on creepy-crawlies?'

Factorella huffed and took her place at the control panel of Factotum, the Fact Cave supercomputer . . .

THE SCIENTIFIC NAME FOR CREEPY-CRAWLIES IS ARTHROPODS. THE ONES YOU'LL BE ENCOUNTERING ARE:

INSECTS: THEY HAVE SIX LEGS, THREE BODY PARTS (HEAD, THORAX AND ABDOMEN), ANTENNAE AND MOST HAVE WINGS. FOR EXAMPLE: BEETLES, GRASSHOPPERS AND FLIES.

MYRIAPODS: THESE ARE CREATURES WITH LONG, SEGMENTED BODIES AND LOTS OF LEGS. FOR EXAMPLE: CENTIPEDES AND MILLIPEDES.

ARACHNIDS: THERE ARE 66,000 SPECIES OF ARACHNIDS, THE SECOND BIGGEST CATEGORY. THEY HAVE FOUR PAIRS OF LEGS, AND NO WINGS OR ANTENNAE. FOR EXAMPLE: SPIDERS, SCORPIONS, TICKS AND MITES.

'Now you know what you're up against, it's time to be shrunk!' exclaimed Professor Miniscule as he took aim with the Shrinkotron . . .

'Don't we have an evening weather forecast to prepare?' pleaded Knowledge. 'I think it's going to be a tricky forecast what with the barometric—'

But before he could finish his sentence Professor Miniscule had pulled the trigger. There was a loud bang and a flash of blue light. Captain Fact and Knowledge had been miniaturised!

'Mind you don't step on them, Factorella!' said Professor Miniscule, as he carefully picked up the shrunken superheroes. 'You're probably wondering how you're going to get around. Well, fear not, for I've got another astonishing invention.'

Professor Miniscule fished around in his lab coat pocket and produced a matchbox.

'We can't get around in a matchbox,' said Captain Fact.

'Can you at least put some wheels on it?' asked Knowledge.

'Don't be ridiculous!' said Professor Miniscule, as he opened the matchbox. 'Behold the Insectopod! It's an all-terrain, jet-powered, submersible, miniature travellator and it's smaller than a cornflake!'

FLAMING THUMB
SAFETY MATCHES

As Captain Fact and Knowledge strapped themselves into the Insectopod and prepared for take off, Professor Miniscule's voice crackled through the intercom.

'I'm still trying to piece together the President's day – *crackle* – unfortunately he's too incoherent to tell the doctors exactly when he got bitten – *fizz* – some creepy-crawly bites are slow acting so it could have been at any point during the day – *whirr* – we do know he woke up feeling itchy – *crackle* – so the first stop is the Presidential Bedroom.'

Losing no time, Captain Fact fired up the Insectopod and buzzed out of the Fact Cave . . .

26

CHAPTER 3
BEDBUGS BITE BACK

AS CAPTAIN FACT and Knowledge whizzed across the city they homed in on their target . . .

'Look, Knowledge, the Presidential Palace,' said Captain Fact. 'Security will be tighter than ever . . .'

As they flew over the heavily guarded compound, Knowledge had an idea. 'The President has a pet cat called Fangleberry,' he said, 'and as we say in the dog world, "Where there's a cat there's a flap" . . .'

Sure enough, Captain Fact spotted a cat flap and the Insectopod swooped through the unguarded entrance.

Narrowly avoiding a swipe from Fangleberry's paw, the Insectopod buzzed up the palace stairs.

'That was close but there's no time to waste. First stop the President's bedroom,' said Captain Fact as they zipped through the keyhole.

'I just saw something move in the bed,' said Knowledge nervously.

'Let's investigate,' said Captain Fact.

30

After landing the Insectopod
on the bedside table Captain
Fact and Knowledge cautiously
slid under the sheets.

'Oh, how cute,' said Knowledge, 'a
family of orange bugs snoozing by the
President's teddy.'

Suddenly an antenna twitched.

'I think we've woken them up,' said Captain Fact
nervously. 'Ker-Fact! Antennae are used to detect
vibrations and smells.'

'But *I* don't smell,' protested Knowledge.

'Never mind that, Knowledge, those are
bedbugs.'

'And?' asked Knowledge.

'And they live on blood! RUN!' cried Captain Fact, and the two superheroes sprinted back to the Insectopod pursued by a ravenous rabble of bed bugs . . .

Safely inside the Insectopod, Captain Fact and Knowledge made for the kitchen.

'Bedbugs give you a nasty nip, enough to make the President itch, but they're not poisonous,' explained Captain Fact. 'There's nowhere in the house creepy-crawlies like better than the kitchen. Maybe we'll find our assailant in there.'

'We need to target the grizzliest part of the kitchen,' said Captain Fact.

'Underneath the fridge,' suggested Knowledge, 'it's amazing what you find down there.'

Captain Fact and Knowledge nervously crept under the gigantic presidential fridge.

'I feel like we're being watched,' said Knowledge.

'We are,' said Captain Fact. Slowly they became aware of dozens of pairs of beady eyes staring at them . . . and a horrid scuttling noise.

'RUN!' screamed Knowledge.

'There's no need to run,' said Captain Fact calmly. 'These cockroaches are harmless.' And with that his ears began to wobble . . .

'Wow!' exclaimed Knowledge, 'I had no idea cockroaches were so amazing!'

'Amazing but not deadly,' said Captain Fact as they retook their seats in the Insectopod.

'So why is it they're so keen to climb aboard?' asked Knowledge as he became aware of a gang of slavering cockroaches salivating over the windscreen.

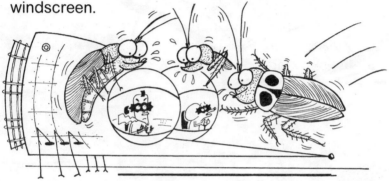

'I think they've sniffed out your canine cookies,' said Captain Fact.

'They're pepperoni-flavoured, my favourite,' said Knowledge.

Suddenly Professor Miniscule crackled through on the intercom. 'Cut the chit-chat – *crackle* – I've just found out that the President always has a pre-breakfast walk in the palace garden – *fizz* – investigate at once – *crackle* – the President is now juggling iced doughnuts and balancing a goldfish bowl on his head . . .'

And so the Insectopod zoomed back through the cat flap and out into the Presidential Garden . . .

CHAPTER 4
BUZZ OFF!

AS CAPTAIN FACT and Knowledge cruised over flower beds and lawns they couldn't believe just how many creepy-crawlies were out and about.

'The place is teeming,' said Captain Fact. 'It's only when you're this teeny that you realise just how many insects there are. Let's get in amongst the daisies and find our bug.'

As the Insectopod weaved its way through the undergrowth, Captain Fact analysed and profiled each creepy-crawly they encountered.

KER-FACT!
LADYBIRDS UNDER ATTACK LET OFF A VILE-SMELLING FLUID.

KER-FACT!
BEES' WINGS BEAT 11,400 TIMES A MINUTE.

KER-FACT!
THERE CAN BE OVER TWO MILLION EARTHWORMS IN JUST ONE HECTARE.

KER-FACT!
EARWIGS GET THEIR NAME
BECAUSE PEOPLE BELIEVED
THAT THEY WOULD CRAWL
INTO YOUR EAR WHEN YOU
WERE ASLEEP AND BORE
INTO YOUR BRAIN.

KER-FACT!
STAG BEETLES AREN'T
VERY GOOD AT FLYING
AND SOMETIMES
CRASH LAND.

KER-FACT!
SLUGS ARE GREAT
CLIMBERS AND CAN
CLIMB UP TO
NINE METRES.

'So none of those are what bit the President,' said Knowledge despondently. 'I knew we'd find nothing dangerous in the garden.'

'Not so fast, Knowledge,' said Captain Fact, thinking hard. 'If we're going to find our creepy-crawly we're going to have to think like a creepy-crawly. Now, if you were the kind of poisonous creepy-crawly who'd bite a President, where would you hide out?'

'On the swings,' said Knowledge, 'they're the best fun you can have in a garden!'

'Don't be ridiculous,' said Captain Fact. 'You'd be lurking in the deepest, darkest, dingiest, most hidden place you could find . . .'

And with that the Insectopod swooped down into an old hollow tree in the very furthest and most overgrown corner of the garden.

'There's nothing here,' said a relieved Knowledge, 'apart from a few woodlice and an old football. I didn't realise the President played soccer.'

'He certainly does,' said Captain Fact, 'he's a pretty good goalie. But that's not a football – it's a hornets' nest!'

Captain Fact only just managed to pull the Insectopod round as an angry swarm of hornets came flying out of the nest.

'Hit the turbo boost, Knowledge,' ordered Captain Fact. 'We've got to get out of here NOW!'

As the Insectopod desperately tried to evade the onrushing hornets, Captain Fact's ears began to throb . . .

'They're gaining on us,' gasped Knowledge, 'we're done for!'

'Not quite, my four-legged friend,' said Captain Fact calmly. 'Ker-Fact! If you're attacked by a swarm of wasps or hornets you should seek cover in some water and remain submerged until they've moved on!'

Within moments the Insectopod had splashed into the Presidential Pond.

SPLOOSH!

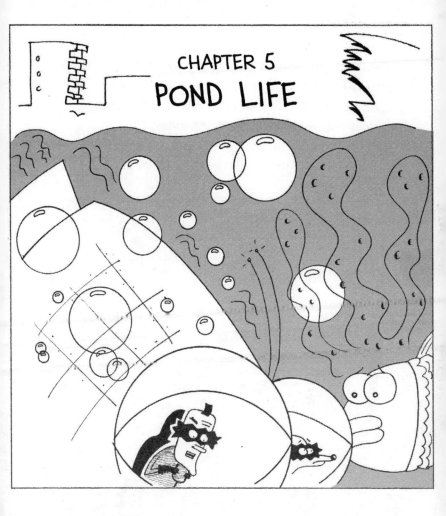

CHAPTER 5
POND LIFE

AS THE INSECTOPOD slipped beneath the surface of the pond the angry hornets returned to their nest.

'Although hornets have a really nasty sting, the symptoms don't match the President's,' said Captain Fact. 'We'd better investigate this pond. DIVE! DIVE! DIVE!'

As the Insectopod plunged deeper, once again Captain Fact scanned the scene in search of the presidential pest. All around him the pond was teeming with watery creepy-crawlies.

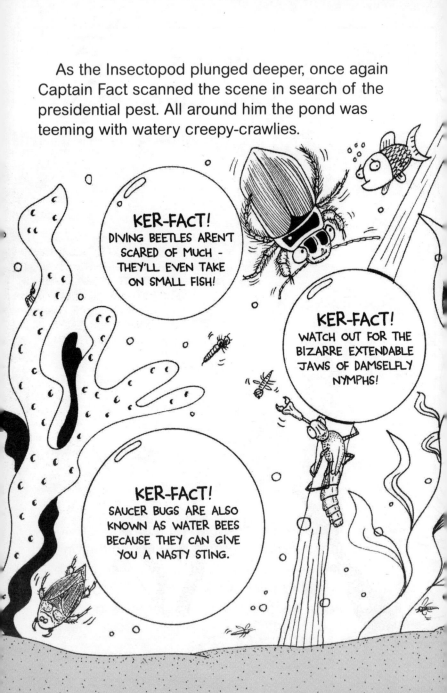

'Well, there are no likely candidates here, Knowledge. Time to surface,' concluded Captain Fact. He gripped the steering column tightly, leaned back and the Insectopod began to ascend from the murky depths.

'Why have we slowed down?' asked Knowledge. 'It feels like an extra passenger has jumped aboard.'

'We *have* got an extra passenger,' said Captain Fact looking up, 'a bloodsucking leech! And he's trying to suck us out! Reverse thrusters to maximum!' But the harder the Insectopod struggled to pull away, the tighter the leech clamped on.

'How can we shake it off?' asked Knowledge.

'Ker-Fact! Leeches are best removed using insect repellent or lemon juice,' said Captain Fact, reaching into his packed lunch. 'Luckily lemonade is my favourite citric beverage.' And with that he emptied the lemonade into the torpedo tubes and fired!

The leech recoiled as it got a stinging squirt of lemonade, releasing the Insectopod.

'Phew,' gasped Knowledge as they surfaced and gently bobbed in the waves. 'Leeches suck!'

Just then they heard a high-pitched drone . . .

'So do mosquitoes,' said Captain Fact as his elbows began to itch . . .

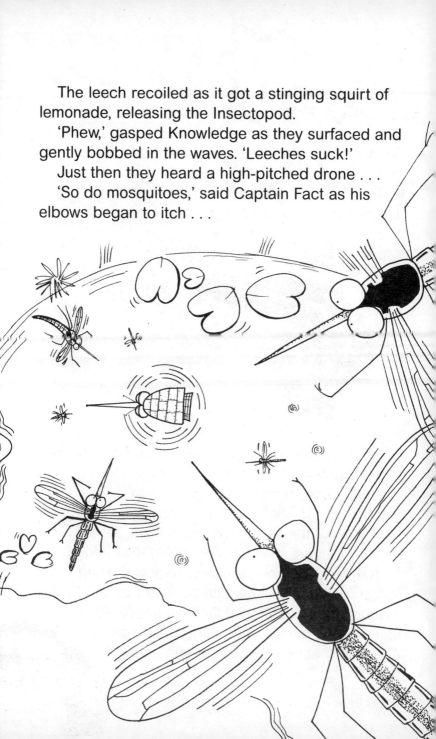

BLOODSUCKER SHAKE

FACT

MOSQUITOES ARE FOUND ALL OVER THE WORLD - EVEN IN THE ARCTIC!

NOSE BURGER ROYALE

FACT

YOU CAN RUN BUT YOU CAN'T HIDE - HUNGRY MOSQUITOES TRACK YOU DOWN BY SIGHT, USING INFRA-RED FROM WARMTH EMITTED BY YOUR BODY, AND BY DETECTING CHEMICALS RELEASED FROM YOUR SKIN AND THE CARBON DIOXIDE IN YOUR BREATH.

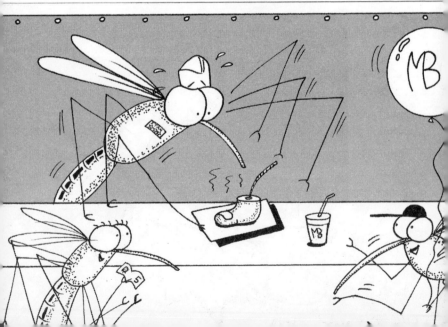

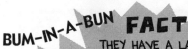

BURGER

with every meal

IT'S MOZZ-TASTIC!

BUM-IN-A-BUN **FACT**

THEY HAVE A LARGE TUBULAR PROBOSCIS (OR NOSE) THAT THEY STICK IN YOU TO SUCK YOUR BLOOD (YUK!).

FRENCH FINGERS

FACT

ONLY FEMALE MOSQUITOES BITE - THEY NEED THE BLOOD FOR THEIR EGGS.

FILET-O-FOOT

FACT

ALTHOUGH MOSQUITO BITES AREN'T FATAL THE GERMS THEY CARRY CAN BE AND MOSQUITOES SPREAD DISEASES LIKE YELLOW FEVER AND MALARIA.

ATTACK!!!

'Nasty!' said Knowledge.

'But not what we're looking for,' said Captain Fact as the intercom sparked into life.

CHAPTER 6
THAT STING THING

WITH THE BOOSTERS set to supersonic the Insectopod buzzed over land and sea until the Sahara desert lay before them . . .

'It's huge!' gasped Knowledge.

'Ker-Fact! The Sahara Desert is the world's biggest desert. Some parts don't get rain for years on end!' said Captain Fact.

Climbing down from the Insectopod Captain Fact and Knowledge nervously surveyed the parched landscape.

'It's boiling out here,' said Knowledge, mopping his brow. 'Surely no creepy-crawly could survive in this heat.'

'That's just where you're wrong,' said Captain Fact as something stirred in the sand. A small head popped up.

'Look, it's a baby creepy-crawly,' said Knowledge affectionately. 'He looks lost. Come to Knowledge. Knowledge has got a lovely doggie snack for you.'

'I wouldn't do that, Knowledge,' said Captain Fact.

'Why not?' asked Knowledge, 'he's so cute . . .'

'Because he's a baby scorpion,' said Captain Fact, 'and they live on their mothers' backs.'

The ground began to shudder and shake.

'He doesn't look so cute now,' snivelled Knowledge.

The ground erupted and staring at them angrily was a huge scorpion.

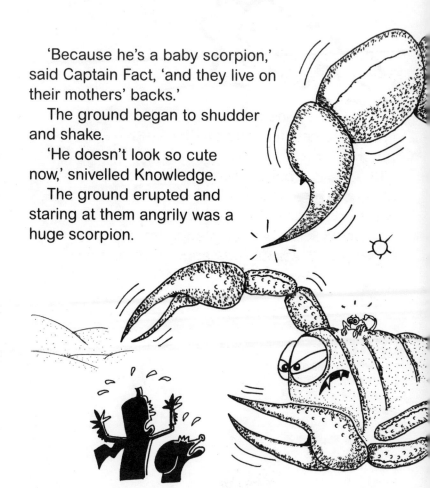

'Time to make ourselves scarce,' yelled Captain Fact. 'Dive for cover!'

As Captain Fact and Knowledge found refuge in a strangely warm pile of mud, Captain Fact's nose began to twitch . . .

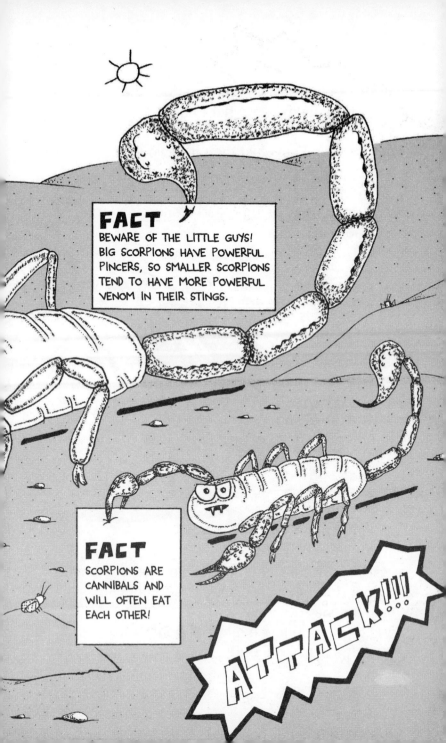

'I don't believe it,' said Knowledge, 'that scorpion didn't want to come anywhere near us.'

'Is it just me, or is there a funny smell in here?' asked Captain Fact. Just then the two superheroes began to judder.

'We're moving!' shrieked Knowledge. And sure enough they were being rolled along by a large, shiny beetle.

'Ker-Fact! It's a dung beetle, they live on camel and goat droppings,' exclaimed Captain Fact. 'Which means . . .'

'We've jumped into a lump of poo!' said Knowledge. 'Let's get out!'

After they'd extracted themselves from the lump of dung the sky suddenly got dark.

'I thought deserts were meant to be dry places,' said Knowledge, 'but it feels like it's going to rain.'

'That's no rain cloud,' explained Captain Fact. 'It's a swarm of desert locusts! I told you there were lots of creepy-crawlies out here. Back to the Insectopod.'

As they sprinted back Captain Fact's forehead began to throb . . .

'Phew! You wouldn't want that lot gatecrashing a picnic,' said Knowledge, as they sat safely in the cockpit of the Insectopod.

Suddenly the intercom spluttered into life.

'Presidential update – the President has now disguised himself as Little Bo Peep and is discussing world politics with an electric toaster – *crackle* – I've just found out that the President and the Brazilian Ambassador meet up once a week to play soccer – *fizz* – they met this morning and the Ambassador had just got back from a trip to Brazil – *pop* – head for the Amazonian rainforest at once!'

CHAPTER 7
RUMBLE IN THE JUNGLE!

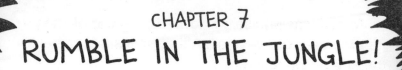

IN NO TIME the turbo-charged Insectopod was buzzing over the Amazonian jungle . . .

'Well, Knowledge, if you think we've met some amazing creepy-crawlies so far, you ain't seen nothing yet,' said Captain Fact ominously.

'Really?' gulped Knowledge as he nervously nibbled a chutney-flavoured dog biscuit.

'Ker-Fact! Over half the animal and plant species found on earth live in jungles.' Captain Fact scanned the forest floor for a suitable place to park.

'There,' said Knowledge, 'a soft fluffy landing spot.'

'Great,' said Captain Fact as he landed the Insectopod. 'And here, take this umbrella.'

As they disembarked they suddenly had the distinct feeling that the ground was moving.

'We're moving,' said Knowledge, 'good of them to provide a bus service. Although it's the hairiest bus I've ever been on!'

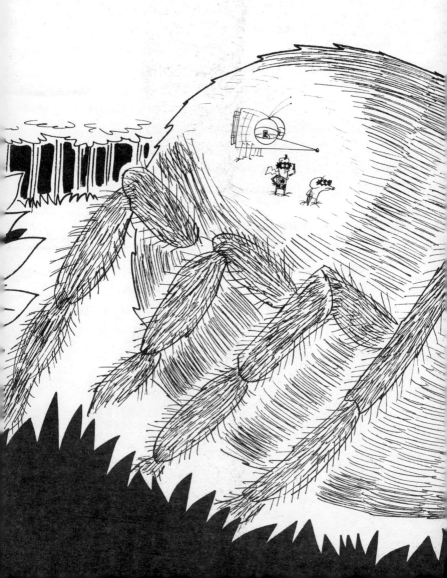

'It's not a bus – it's a tarantula!' explained Captain Fact. 'But there's no need to panic. Ker-Fact! A tarantula's diet is made up of insects, frogs, lizards and mice and they can go without food for months at a time.'

'I still don't like the look of those fangs,' said Knowledge.

'They're used to paralyse prey,' said Captain Fact. 'Not very nice, but not enough to endanger the President.'

Suddenly the tarantula ground to a halt.

'Looks like he's parking up in his burrow,' said Captain Fact. 'Let's see what else is lurking out here.'

All around them was the scurrying and fluttering of many jungle creatures.

'This place is alive with creepy-crawlies,' said Knowledge. 'Our culprit has got to be here.'

Just then a giant millipede poked his head out from behind a half-eaten leaf.

'Quick, open up that umbrella!' shouted Captain Fact.

'But it's not raining,' said Knowledge.

'Just do it!'

As Knowledge opened the umbrella the millipede showered them in a fine venomous spray.

Before Captain Fact could explain the effects of millipede venom they were swept off their feet and carried at great speed across the forest floor . . .

All around them millions of ants were smashing and grabbing anything in their path that looked edible . . . including the Insectopod!

Despite being on his back, and firmly gripped by a mean looking worker ant in a hurry, Captain Fact's chin began to throb . . .

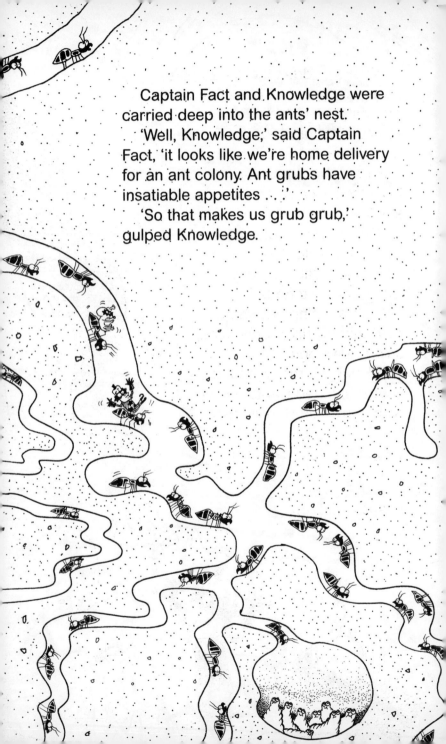

Captain Fact and Knowledge were carried deep into the ants' nest.

'Well, Knowledge,' said Captain Fact, 'it looks like we're home delivery for an ant colony. Ant grubs have insatiable appetites ...'

'So that makes us grub grub,' gulped Knowledge.

All of a sudden there was panic amongst the ants. They began dropping everything and scampering for cover. A long, thin wiggly tongue was waggling around above them and the Insectopod was already stuck to it!

'Quick, this is our chance, it's a giant anteater!' screeched Captain Fact. 'Jump on the tongue!'

'I'm not going anywhere near that horrible slimy thing,' said Knowledge.

'Would you rather be ant soup?' shouted Captain Fact as he grabbed Knowledege and leapt aboard the sticky tongue. With an almighty slurp they were sucked up out of the nest by the hungry anteater.

As Captain Fact had hoped, the anteater didn't fancy a superhero snack and unceremoniously spat them out.

Wet and sticky but otherwise unharmed Captain Fact and Knowledge gratefully got into the Insectopod.

CHAPTER 8
BLUNDER DOWN UNDER

AS THE SUPERHEROES sponged themselves down, the intercom spluttered into life.

'Come in Insectopod – *crackle* – come in Insectopod – there's been a change of plan – *fizz* – I've just discovered that the President was guest of honour at a lunch hosted by the Australian Prime Minister – *pop* – you must proceed at once to Australia – *fizz* . . .'

Without further ado Captain Fact and Knowledge blasted off 'Down Under'.

The Insectopod touched down in Australia, narrowly avoiding being trampled by a mob of kangaroos.

'Ker-Fact! Australia is the world's biggest island continent and home to nearly a quarter of a million types of creepy-crawly,' said Captain Fact clambering out of the Insectopod. 'So there's no time for tangling with the wrong one.'

'Looks like I'm already tangled up in something,' said Knowledge looking down at his paws.

But before you could say 'g'day mate' our two superheroes had been swept up by big hairy legs and bundled into a burrow.

'I heard that Australians were friendly,' said
Knowledge, 'but this is amazing hospitality! Two
complete strangers and we're literally dragged in
for tea!'

'Unfortunately, Knowledge, your new best friend
is a trap door spider and we *are* his tea,' whispered
Captain Fact, as he peered through the gloom and
realised there was no way out.

'Does this mean what I think it means?' asked
Knowledge.

'It certainly
does, Knowledge,'
said Captain Fact and with
that he pressed the emergency
button on his Fact Watch.

Suddenly there was a commotion at the entrance of the trap door spider's lair.

'Looks like some sort of beetle,' said Captain Fact. 'Let's hope the spider finds it more appetising than us.'

Sure enough the trap door spider glanced over his shoulder then eagerly set off to grab the tasty morsel knocking at his door.

'Quick, Knowledge, here's our chance. Let's run for it,' said Captain Fact, grabbing Knowledge and making a bid for freedom.

Outside the burrow the beetle was running rings around the spider. It bounced and flew beyond the reach of its eight hairy legs.

'I didn't know there were beetles made out of metal,' said Knowledge, 'with flowery patterns.'

'That's not a beetle,' said Captain Fact, 'it's Factorella!'

'Hello guys! Isn't this fun?' shouted Factorella. 'Luckily for you, Dad finished building the Beetlebuggy this morning!'

'It's the first time I've ever been pleased to see a creepy-crawly,' said Knowledge. 'I had no idea they could be useful!'

'Actually, Knowledge, only a tiny handful of creepy-crawlies are a nuisance,' said Captain Fact as his shins began to shudder, 'and a lot of them are really very useful . . .'

Factorella's frantic flying had left the trap door spider so dizzy that it was lying on its back with its eyes goggling and head spinning.

'You need to find that creepy-crawly quickly,' said Factorella. 'The President now thinks he's King Kong and is on the palace roof swiping at pigeons. I'd love to help you out but I've got to get back. Dad's washing his moustache and I've borrowed the hairdryer.'

And with that the Beetlebuggy disappeared over the horizon.

'Thanks, Factorella!' said Captain Fact as they boarded Insectopod. 'Right Knowledge, it's now or never. I've got one last idea as to where this creepy-crawly might be lurking . . .'

CHAPTER 9
BIT ON THE BOT!

AS THE INSECTOPOD landed in the Australian Prime Minister's home, Captain Fact knew there was no time to waste.

'Right, Knowledge, we're going straight to the bathroom!'

'Great idea,' said Knowledge. 'A lovely long soak in a hot bath, what could be better after a long day's bug hunting. Did you bring bubble bath?'

But Captain Fact wasn't listening as he boldly went where no man had gone before: into the darkness behind the Prime Minister's toilet. 'Our creepy-crawly has got to be here somewhere,' he said. 'Knowledge, you investigate the plug-hole, I'm going to check out the . . . Knowledge?' But Knowledge was nowhere to be seen.

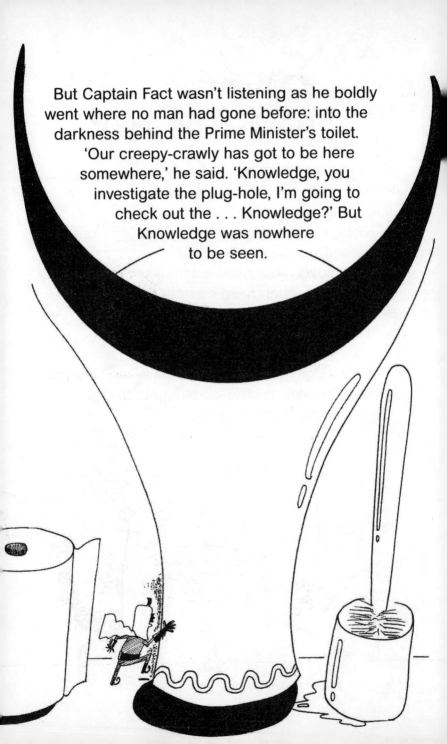

All of a sudden Knowledge came bounding in.

'Captain Fact, look, I'm an aeroplane . . . wheeeee, wheeeee. Your cape looks like a giant banana. I like banana splits, can I have a bite, please? Please?'

'Knowledge, what's happened?' asked Captain Fact as Knowledge started doing handstands whilst reciting doggy poetry.

'I've been bitten by a spider,' said Knowledge as he licked Captain Fact's quiff. 'It was painful at first but now I just feel slightly strange.'

'Where were you bitten?' asked Captain Fact frantically.

'On the bottom, if you must know,' replied Knowledge.

'No, where in the bathroom?'

'Over there by that funnel-shaped web,' said Knowledge.

'That's it, Knowledge, you've cracked it!' shouted Captain Fact. 'Your bottom has just saved the President! Back to the Insectopod at once!'

Captain Fact picked up Knowledge, who was now lying on his back demanding to be tickled, and sprinted to the Insectopod.

'Come in, Professor Miniscule! Come in, Professor Miniscule!'

'Miniscule here. I read you.'

'We've got it' said Captain Fact. 'Well, actually Knowledge has got it. I mean—'

'I don't care who's got it. Just tell me what it is!' demanded Professor Miniscule.

'A Sydney funnel-web spider! That's what bit the President!' said Captain Fact, desperately trying to stay calm. 'Ker-Fact! Its venom attacks the nerves of the body causing muscle twitches, perspiration and tears. It also causes changes to blood vessels, which can affect the brain, leading to shock. This explains the President's strange behaviour.'

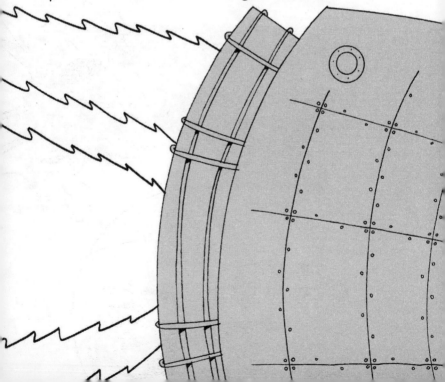

'Of course! – *fizz* – One of the world's most deadly arthropods – *crackle* – fortunately an antivenom for the Sydney funnel-web spider has been around since 1980 – *crackle* – I'll inform the Presidential doctors at once – *wobble* –You've done it! – *crackle* – You've saved the day!'

'What about Knowledge?' asked Captain Fact anxiously. 'He now thinks he's a cup of tea and is demanding to be stirred.'

'Oh, there's some antivenom in the Insectopod first-aid kit – *fizz* – an injection of that will see him right.'

As Captain Fact administered the antivenom his head began to wobble . . .

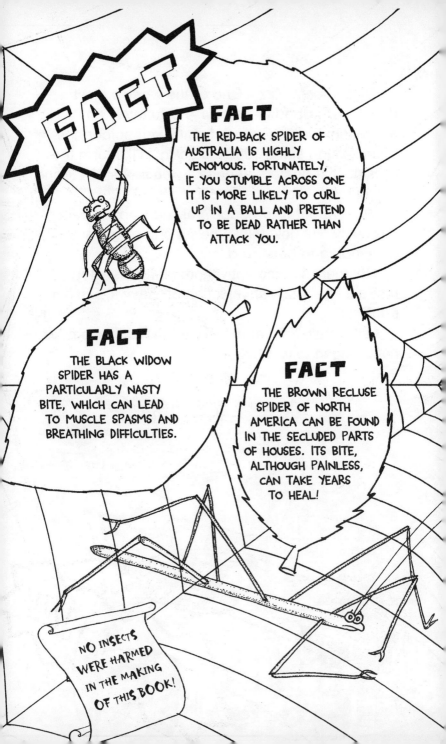

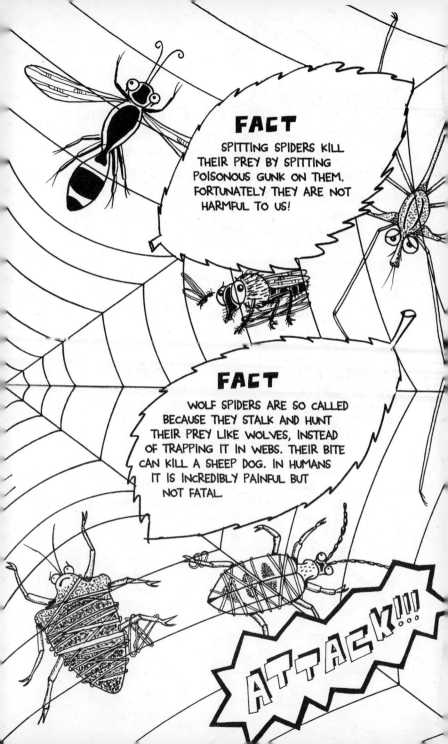

Slowly Knowledge began to come round . . .

'I feel much better. Where am I? Recuperating on one of Australia's stunning beaches? Being looked after by the world's leading spider bite experts?'

'Don't be ridiculous, Knowledge. You're in the Insectopod with me. We're heading home as quickly as we can. Get changed, we've got the evening weather forecast to do!'

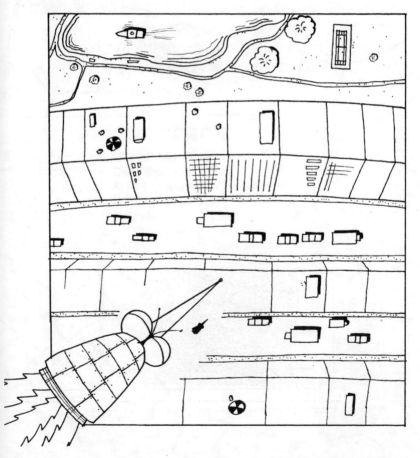

CHAPTER 10
AND NOW THE WEATHER . . .

'COME IN INSECTOPOD – *crackle* – as soon as you're back in your office – *fizz* – you'll eject – *crackle* – then I'll un-shrink you by remote control!' said Professor Miniscule.

'Great!' replied Cliff as he targeted his office window. 'What could possibly go wrong now?'

Just then a gust of wind (that Cliff hadn't forecast) swept them into the wrong office – the Boss's office!

'Professor Miniscule!' screamed Cliff. 'Don't un-shrink us . . .'

But it was too late, there was a pulse of light and a blue flash and Cliff and Puddles found themselves sat on the Boss's lap.

'I must have sunstroke.' said the Boss, dazed and confused, as Cliff and Puddles dashed out of his office. 'I knew I should have had more shade on my mosquito net.'

Cliff and Puddles burst into the Make-up Department.

'There you are,' said Lucy. 'Have you heard the news?'

'No, what's happened?' asked Cliff.

'The President's been saved!' said Lucy. 'If it hadn't been for Captain Fact they might never have worked out what bit him. He only just got the serum in time. I'd love to catch Captain Fact in *my* web . . .'

Cliff blushed as Puddles led him to the studio.

And so with the President safely back at his desk running the country, Cliff Thornhill and Puddles were safely back doing what they did worst – the weather.

Until the next crisis . . .